Animals that Build

Written by Jo Windsor

Some animals can build. This beaver builds a home with logs.

The beaver cuts down
the logs with its teeth.

This squirrel builds a home with grass and twigs.

It makes a nest
for its babies.

Termites build a big nest, too.
They get mud to make the nest.

This termite nest has lots of rooms.

This bird builds a nest with mud.
The nest has two rooms.

This bird builds a nest with bark.

Look at this bird.
This bird builds a nest with grass.

This bird builds a nest with sticks.
It makes a nest in a tree.

This spider builds a nest, too.
It makes a door for the nest.

This spider builds a web with silk.

People build, too.
They can build houses
from lots of things.

Index

beaver 2,3

birds 8–11

people 14

spiders 12,13

squirrel 4,5

termites 6,7

Guide Notes

Title: Animals that Build
Stage: Early (2) – Yellow

Genre: Nonfiction (Expository)
Approach: Guided Reading
Processes: Thinking Critically, Exploring Language, Processing Information
Visual Focus: Photographs (static images)

THINKING CRITICALLY
(sample questions)
- What do you think this book is going to tell us?
- What do you know about animals that build things?
- Focus the children's attention on the Index. Ask: "What animals are you going to find out about in this book?"
- If you want to find out about a beaver, what page would you look on?
- If you want to find out about termites, what page would you look on?
- Look at page 3. How does the beaver cut down logs?
- Look at page 7. Why do you think this termite has a lot of rooms in its nest?
- Look at page 8. What is this bird using to build with?
- Look at page 13. What is the spider using to build with?
- What animal do you think might build the quickest?

EXPLORING LANGUAGE

Terminology
Title, cover, photographs, author, photographers

Vocabulary
Interest words: logs, termites, silk, web
High-frequency words (reinforced): some, can, the, it, has, get, this, with, a, its, for, they, too, makes, look
New words: rooms, two

Print Conventions
Capital letter for sentence beginnings, periods, commas